CONNECTIONS READERS

Love Triangle

CHERYL PAVLIK

Series Editor: John Rosenthal

Boston   Burr Ridge, IL   Dubuque, IA   Madison, WI
New York   San Francisco   St. Louis
Bangkok   Bogotá   Caracas   Lisbon   London   Madrid   Mexico City
Milan   New Delhi   Seoul   Singapore   Sydney   Taipei   Toronto

McGraw-Hill

*A Division of The **McGraw·Hill** Companies*

Connections Readers: Love Triangle

domestic   2 3 4 5 6 7 8 9 0 DOC DOC 9 0 0 9 8
international   2 3 4 5 6 7 8 9 0 DOC DOC 9 0 0 9 8

ISBN 0-07-292788-7

Editorial director: Thalia Dorwick
Publisher: Tim Stookesberry
Development editor: Pam Tiberia
Production supervisor: Richard DeVitto
Print materials consultant: Marilyn Rosenthal
Project manager: Shannon McIntyre, Function Thru Form, Inc.
Design and Electronic Production: Function Thru Form, Inc.
Typeface: Goudy
Printer and Binder: R.R. Donnelley and Sons

Grateful acknowledgment is made for use of the following:
Illustration: © Chris Duke

Library of Congress Catalog Card Number: 97-75582

http://www.mhhe.com

Chapter 1
Back Again!

Ramón was at the after-school program. He was watching a group of children play soccer. He was helping them.

"It's good to be outside with these kids," Ramón thought. "They need a coach, and I need to get out of the restaurant more often."

"Hey, Timmy," Ramón said to one of the kids in the program. "This is soccer. You can't use your hands. Just your feet."

Suddenly Ramón looked up. There was Rebecca! She was back from Boston. Ramón walked over to say hello.

"Rebecca? Are you really here? I don't believe it!" he said. He had a big smile on his face.

"I'm here. I'm really here." Rebecca said. She looked very happy to see him.

He gave her a big hug. "It's great to have you back."

"Oh, it's good to be back."

Then, Alex came running over to them and gave Rebecca another hug.

"Rebecca! You're back! We beat the Hawks! They're the best baseball team in the city!"

"See, I always told you," Rebecca said to him. "You guys are great! Alex, I want to thank you for the nice letter and drawing you sent me. It meant a lot."

Alex was embarrassed. He looked down at his feet. "That's OK. I like drawing anyway."

"Hey . . . your team's waiting for you!" his father said.

"See you later," Alex said as he ran back to his friends.

"So . . . where are you going now?" Ramón asked Rebecca.

"I have a meeting at school with my adviser."

"How are you doing? Really?" Ramón asked.

"Most of the time I'm fine."

"And other times?"

"And other times . . . well . . . I see something and I think, 'I have to tell Dad about that.' Then I remember . . ." Rebecca said. She almost started to cry.

"I know," Ramón said. "It'll be easier. But it takes time."

"The letter from you and Alex meant a lot to me. I didn't want to cry, you know . . ."

"It happened to me when my grandmother died. Alberto and I both cried a lot. I still think about her, but now it doesn't hurt as much."

Rebecca tried to smile.

"So, you're going back to school?" Ramón said.

"Yes. I have to finish school. I'll do anything. But I have to finish."

"Good for you! Are we going to see you around here?"

Rebecca looked serious. "Emma had to find someone to take my place."

"Sorry . . . I was afraid of that . . . But you'll still be giving Alex guitar lessons. And I'm still going to pay for those lessons."

"Good. We can start again next week," Rebecca said.

"We really need you. Alex's guitar sounds terrible! He can't fix it, and I can't help him."

"That's easy. I can fix it in five minutes."

"Well, I guess I should get back to the game," Ramón said.

"Right . . . and I have to go to see my adviser."

"Right . . . maybe Alex and I can buy you an ice cream cone one of these days. You know, when you have time."

Rebecca smiled. "I love ice cream," she said. Then she stopped for a second. "I'll find the time."

Ramón walked back to the game. "Rebecca's back. I can't believe it." He felt very happy. Then he thought of something else.

"I shouldn't get too happy," he thought. "Rebecca didn't come back to San Francisco for me. She came back to go to school. And she still likes Alberto. Maybe Alberto didn't wait for her, but she doesn't know that. I need to find another woman. There are thousands of women in this city!"

Back Again!

After the soccer game, Ramón took Alex home. Alex ran into the kitchen and saw his grandmother.

"Grandma, guess what! Rebecca's back! Rebecca's back! And she's going to start giving me guitar lessons next week!"

His grandmother stopped cooking and turned to him. "That's great, Alex," she said. "Now go and wash your hands. Dinner is almost ready."

Alex ran out of the kitchen, and Ramón walked in. "Hello, Mama," Ramón said. "Thanks for making dinner."

"So Rebecca's back," Mrs. Mendoza said. "Did you talk to her?"

"Yes, I did."

"And . . . ? Did you tell her about your feelings?"

"Well, no. I asked her about her father and her family. She told me about her plans. That's all."

"Oh, Ramón. I am very worried about this."

"Mama, I've told you many, many times—don't worry. I like Rebecca a lot. But she's Alberto's girlfriend. So, that's that. I'm going to look for another woman. There are thousands of women in San Francisco. There has to be one for me. So stop worrying, Mama. I'm fine. See?"

He kissed his mother. "So what's for dinner?" he asked.

"A new chicken dish. It has very little fat. But don't tell Papa."

"Why?"

"Because you know your father. The doctor wants him to eat less fat, but he won't do it. He says food without fat tastes terrible. He wants to eat like his father. His father lived for 92 years. And his grandfather lived for 91 years."

"But they both worked very hard, and they exercised a lot."

"I know. But you can't tell your father that. He doesn't want to hear it. He just wants to eat his favorite foods. Yesterday he told me, 'If the chef is too thin, people won't eat at the restaurant.' "

"Yes, but Papa isn't the chef anymore. And you're retired."

"I know. I told him that."

"Well, Papa has always been stubborn."

"That's why I married him," Mrs. Mendoza said. "When we were young, I didn't want to go to the United States with your father. But he wouldn't listen. Finally I agreed. And you know the rest of the story."

"Yes," Ramón said. "It has a happy ending. But you don't have to cook without any fat. Just use more vegetables and less cheese."

Suddenly they heard a voice from the dining room. It was Mr. Mendoza.

"Carmen, Ramón, what are you doing in there? Alex and I are very hungry!"

"Just a minute. We'll be right there," Mrs. Mendoza said.

Then Mrs. Mendoza spoke quietly to Ramón. "Listen, tonight's dinner has very little fat. But if we tell Papa, he won't eat it. Let him taste it first. He might like it."

Ramón hugged his mother. "Don't worry, Mama. I won't tell Papa our little secret. And the chicken smells delicious."

Ramón and his mother took the food to the table.

"What are we eating?" Mr. Mendoza asked.

"Something new," she said.

Ramón looked at his father. He didn't look happy.

"It's from Ana. She learned it at cooking school. She calls it chicken Michoacana," Ramón said quickly.

"Chicken Michoacana? I've never heard of it."

"I know. I've never heard of it either," Ramón said. "But it's not really new. It's a traditional dish from the state of Michoacán. I wanted to try it here. If it's good, I might put it on the menu at the restaurant."

"You're going to change the menu?" Mr. Mendoza asked.

"I'm not sure. I'm just thinking about it," Ramón said as he smiled at his mother.

Chapter 2
A Great Dinner and a Good Talk

Ramón and Fernando were in the kitchen. They were ordering the food for the week.

"How many chickens do we need?" Ramón asked.

"Let's see. About 50, I think."

"Maybe we should get a few more," Ramón said. "I tried a new chicken dish last night. I want to put it on the menu. It can be a special, on weekends only."

"What kind of chicken dish is it?" Fernando asked. "Where is it from?"

"Well, it's from my mother. She made it for dinner."

"Well, what should we call it? How about Carmen's chicken?"

"No, its name is Chicken Michoacana."

Suddenly the telephone rang. Ramón answered it.

"Casa Mendoza. Can I help you?"

"Ramón? This is Diana Cruz. Graci's daughter."

"Of course, Diana. How could I forget you? Are you back in town?"

"Yes, I am. I'm home for Christmas. I was wondering . . . Would you like to go out some night this week?"

"Sure. That would be great. I have an idea. There's a new restaurant in town. I haven't been there before, but everyone loves it. They have great fish and a wonderful view of San Francisco Bay and the Bay Bridge."

"That sounds great."

"Are you free tomorrow night?" Ramón asked.

"Sure, but don't you have to work?"

"No. I can take the night off if I want. I have a new manager at the restaurant. I don't have to work so hard anymore."

"That's wonderful news."

"So I'll pick you up at seven o'clock. Is that OK?"

"That's perfect. I'll see you then."

Ramón hung up the telephone.

"Do you mind?" Ramón asked Fernando. "You'll be alone here tomorrow night."

"No, that's OK. I can do it. We'll be fine."

* * *

The next morning, Ramón walked into the kitchen. His parents were eating breakfast.

"Good morning, Ramón," Mr. Mendoza said.

"Good morning, Papa, Mama."

"So what did Diana want yesterday?"

"How did you know about Diana?" Ramón asked.

"She called here first. I told her to call the restaurant."

"She's in town. She wants to see me. We're going to dinner tonight."

"Oh, you are. I can't believe it. I have to call her mother." Mrs. Mendoza stood up and started walking to the phone.

"Mama, don't call anyone. Diana and I are just friends. I told you that before."

Mrs. Mendoza sat down again. "OK. I won't call her. I'm just happy. That's all. She's such a nice girl."

"Woman, Mama, woman. She's not a girl. She's 26 years old."

"OK. She's such a nice woman."

Ramón smiled at his mother. "That's better."

"So where are you taking her?"

"Oh, we're going to the Bayside Bistro. People say it's very good."

"That's nice. Ramón, you're friends now, but it could become something more. Please give this relationship a chance."

"OK, Mama. I promise. I'll give it a chance."

* * *

That night, Ramón and Diana walked into the restaurant. There were a lot of people waiting for tables.

"Look at all these people," Diana said. "The food must be good here. But we'll have to wait for an hour."

"Don't worry. I have already taken care of everything."

Ramón went to speak to the head waiter. A minute later, the waiter came and took them to a table right next to a large window. "How did you do that?" Diana asked. "The sign said: 'No reservations.'"

"I know the owner. He and my father are old friends. He saved this table for us."

"Please thank him for me. It's just perfect—the bridge, the lights, the water. What a great view!"

"Well, you've been in Italy for four months. I wanted to take you somewhere very special."

"You chose very well, Ramón."

"So how is Italy?" he asked.

"Great! My art classes are wonderful. I love every minute of my life there. I want to stay for a long, long time."

"Oh, I'm very happy for you."

"And how about you, Ramón? How are you? You weren't very happy when I saw you in August."

"No, I wasn't. But it's getting better. As I told you, I found a new manager for the restaurant. He's going to start in January, but he's already doing more. So, I can spend some time away from the restaurant. My life is a lot better now."

"That's good."

"Are you married yet?"

"Married?" she laughed. "No, not yet. But my mother still has hopes."

"You haven't met a wonderful young Italian man yet? You aren't sipping coffee and listening to opera with a Giorgio or a Giovanni?" Ramón said with a smile.

"Well, I have two or three men in my life right now. But I'm not ready to be serious about anyone. I just go out and have a good time."

"Is your mother unhappy about that?" he asked.

"Of course! Now she wants little Italian grandchildren."

"Grandchildren!" Ramón cried. "But you're not even married yet."

"I know. But my mother thinks I should have children right away, too."

"I guess I'm lucky," Ramón said. "My mother doesn't bother me about grandchildren. She already has Alex."

"That makes it easier for her, but it must be harder for you," Diana said.

Ramón didn't say anything. He just looked out the window for a minute.

"I'm sorry, Ramón. Did I say something wrong?"

"No, it's just that . . . well . . . my mother does understand something about me."

"What do you mean?"

"There's a woman in my life. Well, not exactly in my life . . . she's . . . well . . ."

"Ramón, what are you trying to say?"

"This woman. Her name is Rebecca. She's my brother Alberto's girl-friend. He met her last summer . . ."

Ramón told her the story.

"And you're in love with her?" Diana asked.

"I think so."

"I see. That is difficult. Does she know about your feelings?"

"Well, I've never told her."

"How does she feel?"

"I'm not sure. Sometimes I think she feels the same way. Other times I just don't know."

"How well do you know her?"

"Not that well. She sees Alex every day. I see her for a few minutes when I pick him up from his after-school program. But I think I understand her better than Alberto does."

"So, what are you going to do?"

"I don't know. Probably nothing."

"Maybe you should wait a few weeks. Maybe her relationship with Alberto will change. He hasn't seen her for a while."

"That's true. It could change. Alberto doesn't have many long relation-ships with women."

After dinner, Ramón drove Diana home. They sat in his car and talked for a while.

"Thanks so much for listening, Diana."

"No problem, Ramón."

"Hey, I just thought of something. I'm going to be in my friend Tony's wedding next week. I don't have a date. Would you like to go with me? It's going to be a great party."

"I'd love it. Wait until our mothers hear this! They'll go crazy!"

They both laughed.

Chapter 3
The Wedding

It was 11:30 A.M. on the day of Tony's wedding. It was also the day of the father-kids football game. Ramón had to go to Tony's wedding. So he couldn't go to the football game. Alberto would take Alex. Alex was happy about the game, but he was sad because Ramón couldn't come.

"You two will have a great time," Ramón said. "It'll be a lot of fun."

"I know, Dad. Are you going to have fun?"

"I hope so. Some weddings aren't very much fun. But this is going to be a small wedding. So Tony and Marilyn can talk to everybody."

They went downstairs. Alberto was waiting for them in the living room.

"Hey, Uncle Alberto," Alex said.

Alberto got up. He threw a football into the air and caught it. "So are you all ready, Alex?"

"Yeah," Alex said. "Uncle Alberto, throw me the ball."

Alberto started to throw the ball, but Ramón stopped him.

"Not in the house, guys. Mama will kill us if we break something."

"Your dad's right," Alberto said. "Remember when we broke the kitchen window?" He laughed.

Ramón laughed, too. "Yeah, Mama was mad for a week. She wouldn't let us go anywhere except school. She grounded us for a long time."

"We can throw the ball outside," Alberto said. "We need to go anyway.

We don't want to be late." He looked at Ramón. "Do you want to throw the ball with us before we go?"

"No, I shouldn't. I have to get ready for the wedding."

"OK. Bye, Dad." Alex kissed his father goodbye.

"Have a good time, you two," Ramón said.

After they left, Ramón went into the kitchen. His parents were eating lunch.

"Do you want some lunch, Ramón?" his mother asked.

"No, I should go. I'm going to meet Tony at his mother's house. Then he and I are going to have lunch alone. It's a little crazy at his house today."

"That's a good idea," his mother said.

"I'll be back pretty late, I think. So don't wait up for me."

"Goodbye, Son," Mr. Mendoza said. "Have a good time."

* * *

Ramón and Tony ate lunch at a quiet restaurant.

"Thanks a lot, Ramón. I needed to get out of Mom's house. She wouldn't leave me alone. And my house is worse. Marilyn and all her friends are there."

"I'm your best man. Taking care of you is part of my job."

"Hey, do you have the wedding rings?"

"Yes, I do. They're right here."

Ramón took a small box out of his pocket and showed it to Tony.

"Great. Now, we should probably go back and get dressed. Do you need to take a shower?" Tony asked.

"No, I took a shower at home. I just need to put my good clothes on."

"Do you have our flowers?" Tony asked.

"Yes, I do. They're in your mother's kitchen."

* * *

Tony and Ramón went to Tony's mother's house and put on their good clothes. At three o'clock, they walked downstairs. Suddenly the telephone rang. Tony's sister, Connie, answered it.

"Tony it's for you. It's Marilyn," she said.

"He can't talk to her before the wedding," Tony's mother said. "It's bad luck."

"Don't be silly, Mom," Tony said. "I can't see her before the wedding. That's bad luck. But I *can* talk to her on the phone."

Tony talked on the phone for a few minutes. "Don't worry, Marilyn. Ramón is taking care of everything. See you soon." Tony put down the telephone.

"What did she want?" Ramón asked.

"She was worried about the rings and the flowers," Tony said, laughing.

"Hey, I just remembered. Don't you have to get Diana?"

"No, her father is driving her to the church," Ramón said. "We're going to meet there."

"That's good. You don't have to worry about that."

"And the boys are with Jane, right?" Ramón asked.

"Yes, she's going to bring them to the church at 3:30."

"Well, we're ready. Let's get the flowers and go."

Ramón went into the kitchen to get the flowers.

"Here, let me help you with those," Connie said.

She put one flower on Tony's jacket and another on Ramón's jacket.

"You two look great," she said. "Take the box. The boys' flowers are still in there."

Tony kissed her goodbye. "OK, Connie. Thanks for everything. See you soon."

"Don't worry. We'll all be there."

Tony and Ramón drove to the church and went inside. There were pink and white flowers everywhere.

"It looks great," Ramón said.

"It should. The flowers weren't cheap. But you only get married once . . ." He stopped for a second. "Or twice."

Just then, Tony's ex-wife came in with their two young sons, Sam and Mark. "Hi, Tony. Hi, Ramón," she said. "Tony, Sam's a little worried. So say something nice to him."

"Don't worry, I will," Tony answered.

"The boys are going home with Connie, right?" she asked.

"Yeah. She'll take them back to your house tomorrow afternoon."

"Fine. I'll be home all afternoon, so she can come any time."

"Thanks, Jane. I'll tell her."

"OK. Well, I should go. Tony, good luck," Jane said. She gave him a hug. Then she left.

"You and Jane still have a good relationship," Ramón said. "That's nice. I want to be friends with Christine, but we always fight."

"We haven't always been so friendly," Tony said. "But you're right. This way is much nicer. And it's easier for the boys."

Tony's sister and his two sons walked up to him.

"Now, what are you going to say to each guest, Sam?"

"Good afternoon. Are you here for the br-, the br-," Sam said, but he couldn't remember the word.

"The bride," Tony said. "That's Marilyn. And the groom, that's me."

"Good afternoon," Sam repeated. "Are you here for the *gribe* or the *broom?*"

Tony laughed. Sam looked upset. "Listen, I have a better idea. Just say, 'Are you Marilyn's friend or Tony's friend?'"

"Good afternoon. Are you Marilyn's friend or Tony's friend?" Sam said proudly.

"That's right. And then what do *you* do, Mark?"

"I put your friends on the right, and Marilyn's friends on the left."

"That's right. The bride's friends and family sit on the left. The groom's friends and family sit on the right," Tony said.

"We should go and wait in the back room now," Ramón said. "People are starting to arrive."

"Do you have the rings?" Tony asked again.

"Yes, Tony. They're right here in my pocket," Ramón said. He laughed.

"OK, bye, guys," Tony said to his sons.

About 20 minutes later, Connie came to the back room. "Marilyn is here. You should come out now."

Tony and Ramón walked to the front of the church. They waited for Marilyn. One of Marilyn's friends walked to the front of the church.

Ramón looked at her. "Who is Marilyn's maid of honor?" Ramón asked quietly.

"She's a friend from the newspaper," Tony said in a low voice.

Then the music changed and Marilyn came into the church. Everybody turned to look at her. She was wearing a beautiful, long white dress. She was carrying pink and white flowers.

"She looks beautiful," Ramón thought. "Tony's a lucky guy. I wonder . . . Will I ever get married again?"

Chapter 4
The Party After the Wedding

After the wedding, Marilyn and Tony went outside the church. Then everybody else came out. Everybody wanted to kiss the bride. And Tony and Marilyn wanted to say hello to all their friends.

A lot of people came up to Ramón and shook his hand or hugged him. Ramón didn't know many of them. But he smiled and shook hands. Some of the people were from Tony's family. He had a large Italian family, with many, many aunts, uncles, and cousins. Some of the guests were Marilyn's friends from the newspaper.

Suddenly Ramón saw Diana.

"Finally, somebody I know," Ramón said. He kissed her. "I've met about 50 people and already, I can't remember their names."

"Don't worry, Ramón," Diana said. "They won't remember your name either." They both laughed.

"It was a nice wedding," Diana said.

"It was great," Ramón said. "And I didn't forget anything. Listen, I have to say hello to a few more people. But then we can drive to the party together."

"Don't you have to go with Tony and Marilyn?" she asked.

"No," Ramón said. "They're going in the limousine." Ramón pointed to a big, long black car. "They want to be alone anyway."

"OK. I'll wait for you," Diana said.

Later Ramón and Diana drove to the party. They talked about the wedding.

"It was nice because it wasn't too big," Diana said.

"Yeah. That was good. Both Marilyn and Tony wanted a small wedding. His mother was upset because she couldn't ask everyone in her family."

"Did you have a big wedding when you got married?" Diana asked.

"Yes," Ramón said. "And I would never do it again. If I get married again, I'm not going to tell anyone. Weddings are a lot of trouble."

"Well, good luck finding a woman. Most women wouldn't agree with you. They like weddings."

"I know. But I don't understand it. You have to plan for a long time and spend a lot of money. For what? I'd rather spend the money on a honeymoon to Hawaii."

"Hawaii's very nice," Diana said. "But then you'd have to come home to your mother, and she'd be very upset."

"You're right," Ramón said. "OK, I'll have a wedding, and my mother can come. But it'll still be a small wedding. Maybe 20 people. No more than that."

"Well, there you are, Ramón. Your wedding is all ready. Now you just need the bride."

Ramón and Diana both laughed.

Ramón parked at the hotel. They went inside and went up the 25th floor. A lot of the guests were already in the room. They were standing and talking. But Tony and Marilyn weren't in the room.

"Where are we sitting?" Diana asked.

"We're at the head table with Marilyn and Tony. Hey, where are they?" Ramón asked. "They left the church before we did, and they're not here."

"Did you take the wedding pictures before the wedding?" Diana asked.

"The wedding pictures!" Ramón cried. "Uh-oh. I forgot the wedding pictures! Tony told me to meet them in Room 1018. I'll be right back!"

"Don't worry, Ramón. I'll be fine," she said.

Half an hour later, Ramón returned with Tony, Marilyn, and Marilyn's maid of honor. Diana was talking to a man.

"I'm really sorry, Diana," Ramón said.

"Don't worry about it. I've been talking to Tony's Uncle Nick."

Ramón and Nick shook hands.

"Are you from San Francisco?" Ramón asked.

"Oh, no. I'm from Denver. I sold used cars there for almost 40 years. Nick's Nice Cars. That was the name of my business. Now my son Nate is going to take over the business. I'm retiring. After 40 years, I've had enough.

It's time for me to sit back and let Nate run the place. He's going to change the name, though. Nate's Nice Cars. He's a good boy. He'll do a fine job. And me, I'm just going to sit back and rest. My wife, Frannie, and I are going to retire and have a good time. We're thinking about moving to Florida, maybe Miami. You know, it's cold in Denver. We've had enough cold weather. We lived in Denver for 60 years. I want to go live in the sun. We're thinking about going to Italy. I'd like to see the old country just once before I die. I was just telling Diana . . ."

Just then, Tony hit a glass with a knife two or three times. It made a loud ringing sound. Everybody stopped talking.

"I want to welcome everybody to our reception. We've planned a great party. So please find your tables."

"Oh, it's time to eat," Nick said. "I'll see you later. Nice talking to you Diana."

Ramón and Diana just looked at each other.

"Did you have a chance to say anything, Diana?" Ramón laughed.

"I told him my name, but not much more. He really likes to talk."

Ramón and Diana sat at a table with Tony and Marilyn, Marilyn's maid of honor, Paula, and Paula's friend Jim. Everybody found his table. Then the singer in the band started to speak.

"Good evening everyone. Now, Tony and Marilyn are going to have their first dance as husband and wife."

The band started to play, and Marilyn and Tony started to dance. After a few minutes, Tony asked Marilyn's mother to dance, and Marilyn asked Tony's father. Soon everyone was dancing. The dancing continued for about half an hour.

Then people went to their tables again and ate dinner. After dinner, Ramón hit a glass with a knife. Everybody was quiet. All the guests looked at him. "I'm Ramón Mendoza. I'm Tony's best man. Well, at least I tried to be his best man."

Everybody laughed. "I'm just kidding," Ramón said. "I've known Tony for 20 years. He and I were in the restaurant business together. Tony was a terrible restaurant owner."

Everybody laughed again.

"But that's a good thing, because Tony cares about his family and friends too much. They were more important to him than a restaurant. Tony made the right decision . . . for him. He sold his restaurant. He's lucky. And so is Marilyn."

Ramón turned to look at Marilyn. "Marilyn, he's a good man. I know you will both be happy together." Ramón lifted his glass and drank from it. Everyone held up their glasses and drank, too.

Ramón sat down again. "That's it," he said. "I've done all my best man jobs."

Then Marilyn and Tony cut the wedding cake together. Marilyn took a fork and fed Tony a piece of cake. Then Tony fed Marilyn a piece of cake.

Later, many of the young women walked to the middle of the dance floor.

"Come on, Diana," Connie said. "Marilyn's going to throw her flowers. If you catch them, you'll get married soon."

"Thanks, but I don't want to get married. If I catch the flowers, my mother will never stop talking about a wedding for me."

"You must be Italian," Connie said.

"No, I'm Mexican, but Italian mothers are a lot like Mexican mothers."

Both women laughed.

"If you catch them, you can give them to me," Connie said.

Marilyn threw her flowers into the air. Diana didn't catch them; neither did Connie.

"Now I can tell my mother the truth," Diana thought.

Chapter 5
Christmas Plans

The day after the wedding, Ramón got up late. When he went downstairs, his mother and Alex were in the kitchen. Alex was wearing a new hat. The hat said "San Francisco 49ers."

"Dad, Dad, you're up," Alex said. "We won! We won! Look at the cool hat. Everybody on the winning team got hats."

Ramón hugged his son. "That's great! Congratulations! Sorry I missed you last night. You were sleeping when I got home."

"Did you have a good time at the wedding?" Alex asked.

"Yeah," Ramón said. "And it sounds like you had a good time at the football game."

"Yeah, Uncle Alberto was great. He and I made the winning play. He threw me the ball, and I ran all the way to the end. We won the game! Uncle Alberto said I was really good. I want to be a football player!"

"What about baseball?" Ramón asked. "Last week you wanted to be a baseball player."

"Baseball's over now, Dad. It's time for football. Can we throw the ball outside now?"

"Wait a minute, Alex. I just got up. Can I have my coffee first?"

"OK. I'll wait for you outside."

Alex ran out of the kitchen.

"Let me make you some breakfast, Ramón," his mother said.

"It's OK, Mama. I just need some coffee."

He walked into the kitchen, and she went with him.

"Sit down and tell me about the wedding. I'll make the coffee."

Ramón sat down at the table.

"The wedding was very nice. There were pink and white flowers in the church. Marilyn's dress was beautiful. And the dinner was . . ."

"That's nice, Ramón, but I want to hear about you and Diana."

"Diana and I had a very nice time. We ate, we danced, we talked, we laughed, and then I took her home."

"So, when are you going to see her again?"

"I don't know. She might come home for the summer. She doesn't want to be in Italy in the summer. She said there are too many Americans in the summer." Ramón laughed.

"Next summer? What about next week?"

"Next week is Christmas, Mama. She has plans with her family. We're both too busy."

"Well, did you ask her to the New Year's party?"

"No, I didn't. She's going back to Italy on the 28th. She won't be here for New Year's."

"But if you asked her, she might stay."

"I don't think so. She already has a date for New Year's Eve. In Italy."

"Oh, no. Graciela is going to be very upset. She really hoped . . ."

"Mama, I told you. We're just friends. Diana told her mother, too. But you wouldn't believe us."

"We just didn't *want* to believe you. We're worried about our children. That's all."

"Well, doña Graciela doesn't have to worry. Diana is just fine. She's very happy. She loves her work, and she loves her life. She's having a great time."

"And you? Should I worry about you?"

"Mama, not again. I'm fine, too. My life is getting better. I had a great time at Tony's wedding last night. And Fernando is going to be the manager in January, so I won't have to work so much. I'm already spending more time outside the restaurant. I coach the soccer team at Alex's after-school program. I'm going out more at night. What are you worried about?"

"Christmas."

"Christmas?"

"Yes. Your father and I are going to Mexico. Alex will be in Los Angeles with his mother. Alberto's going skiing. But you'll be alone on Christmas. You shouldn't be alone on Christmas."

"Mama, I won't be alone. Fernando and Ana will be here."

"They're not family."

"Alberto won't be with family either."

"Rebecca is going with him, I think. He'll be with her. That's different."

"So what should I do?"

"Close the restaurant and come to Mexico with us."

"I can't do that," Ramón said. "We have the Mendoza Christmas tradition."

"I know," Mrs. Mendoza said.

"We always take food to the community center on Christmas."

"Can't somebody else do it?"

"No. Fernando is spending Christmas with his children. Ana is going to her cousin's house after she cooks the food. I'm just taking it to the community center."

"Well, why can't—"

Ramón stopped her. "Mama, I'm not going to talk about this anymore. The people at the community center are expecting Christmas dinner, and I'm going to bring it to them. That's their only Christmas present. That's what Christmas really means—doing something for other people."

"Well, you could go away the day after Christmas. You could go skiing with your brother."

"Mama, I can't go with Alberto and Rebecca! They want to be alone. They don't need me there. And I don't like to ski."

"I just don't want you to be here all alone."

"Listen, I promise you. If I get lonely, I'll call one of my friends."

"Who?"

"I'll call Tony."

"Tony's in Mexico with Marilyn. They're on their honeymoon."

"He'll be back Christmas Day. Or I'll call somebody else."

Alex came to the kitchen door. He was holding a football in his hand. "Dad, can we throw the ball now?" he asked.

Ramón smiled. "Sure, Alex." He drank the rest of his coffee. "Let me get my shoes, and we'll go," he said.

"I'll get them," Alex said. He turned around and ran out of the kitchen.

Chapter 6
Ramón Changes his Plans

Ramón and Alex threw the football for a while. Ramón was talking to Alex, but he was thinking about his mother's words. "She's right," he thought. "I don't want to be alone at Christmas. Well, maybe I'll call a friend. Now who can I call?" he wondered.

"I can't call Tony. He's going to be with Marilyn and his kids on Christmas. It'll be their first holiday as a real family. I can't call Jack. He's going away. I can't call Ernesto. He's going to be with his family. Everybody is always with their family on Christmas. What am I going to do?"

He started to think about a trip. "Maybe the people at the community center could pick up the food at the restaurant," Ramón thought. "That wouldn't be so bad. It's still free food. Ana is cooking it, so it'll be good. But they don't really need me to put it on the plates. Anybody can do that. Maybe I *should* go away."

"But where? I don't want to go to Mexico with Mama and Papa. They'll want to introduce me to every cousin in the world. I won't get any rest. That would be a real family Christmas, but it would be *too much* family. I can't go skiing with Alberto, either. That would be really strange—me, Alberto, and Rebecca on the same mountain."

Then he had an idea. "I know. What about that little hotel in Santa

Barbara? Christine and I loved it there. I could go swimming and just rest. It's a wonderful place. The food is great, the ocean is wonderful, and the rooms are perfect. Is it too late to plan a trip?" he wondered.

The next morning, he was still thinking about going to Santa Barbara. When he got to the restuarant, he picked up the phone. "Maybe I'll try to get a room there. If I can get a room, I'll go. If I can't, I won't go," he thought.

Ramón called his mother's vacation planner. A woman answered the phone.

"Travel Time. Milly speaking. Can I help you?"

"Hi, Milly. This is Ramón Mendoza, Carmen's son."

"Yes, Mr. Mendoza. Would you like that ticket to Monterrey, Mexico?"

"What ticket?"

"Your mother asked me to get another ticket for her flight. She thought you might go with them."

Ramón laughed to himself. "No, Milly. I don't need that ticket, but I would like you to check something for me. Can you get me a room at the Anderson Hotel in Santa Barbara next week?"

"Next week?" Milly was surprised. "You mean Christmas?"

"Yeah," Ramón said. He felt a little bit silly. "Just for three nights—the 24th, 25th, and 26th."

"I'll try, Mr. Mendoza. But it's very late. They're probably full."

"I know. It's probably a stupid idea, but maybe they have something. Maybe somebody changed his plans. Can you check for me? The price isn't important."

"I'll look," Milly said. "But I don't expect to find much. Should I try any other hotels on Santa Barbara?"

"Sure. But I prefer the Anderson Hotel."

"OK, Mr. Mendoza. I'll let you know later today."

"Thanks a lot."

"Oh, and are you sure about the ticket to Monterrey?"

"Yes, I'm sure. I won't need it."

"OK then. I'll talk to you later. Goodbye."

"Goodbye."

Ramón put the phone down.

Fernando and Ana arrived at the restaurant. "Good morning!" he said to them.

"Good morning, Ramón," Fernando said. "It's cold today. It's snowing in the mountains."

"I want to see snow. I've never seen it," Ana said.

"Well, you don't have to go very far to see it," Ramón said. "Just go to the mountains."

"I'll ask my cousin," Ana said "We can go one day when the restaurant is closed."

"That's a good idea," Fernando said. "Or you can learn to ski."

"No, skiing is too expensive," she said. "And I don't want to stay in the snow. I just want to see it. I don't like the cold. I prefer the ocean."

"Oh, I need to talk to you both about something. I'm thinking about taking a short vacation."

"That's fine, Ramón. We can take care of everything."

"I know. I'm not worried about the restaurant. But here's the problem. I want to go away for Christmas. But I promised to help at the community center on Christmas Day."

"There's no problem, Ramón," Fernando said. "I'll help Ana cook, and then we can take the food to the community center together. Right, Ana?"

"No problem," Ana said.

"Can you do that? I know Christmas Day is important. You probably want to spend the day with your families."

"Ramón, sometimes you act too much like an American," Fernando said. "Christmas Day isn't important. Didn't you ever have Christmas in Mexico? December 24th, Christmas Eve, is the important day, not the 25th. We have our Christmas dinner on Christmas Eve. Then at midnight, we open our presents. We don't do anything on Christmas Day."

"It's the same in my family," Ana said. "I usually just sleep on Christmas Day. I'm going to my cousin's house for Christmas dinner on the 24th. I'm not doing anything on the 25th."

"What time is Christmas dinner at the community center?" Fernando asked.

"It's in the afternoon," Ramón said.

"So I'll cook in the morning, and we'll take the food to the community center in the afternoon. That's easy," Ana said.

"We usually stay and put the food on the plates, but you don't have to do that. We can pick up the dirty plates another day."

"That's easy. I can go back and pick them up on the 26th. You see, there's no problem," Fernando said. He was smiling.

"Well, thank you. That's very nice. I feel much better. Anyway, I may not be going. I'm still trying to find a hotel room."

"Where are you going?" Ana asked.

"I want to go to Santa Barbara. I went there once before, and I loved it."

"You don't want to be with your family on Christmas?" Ana asked.

"No, I do. But they're all going away. My parents are going to Mexico, Alex is going to Los Angeles, and Alberto's going skiing. So I'll be alone on Christmas."

"That's too bad," Fernando said. "You can come to my house for Christmas," Fernando said. "It'll be just me and my wife and our kids."

"Yeah, or you can come to Miguel's," Ana said. "He's having a big dinner. He won't mind one more person."

"That's very nice," Ramón said. "Thank you both. I'll let you know."

Ramón walked to his office. He saw a note on his desk. It was the menu for the dinner at the community center. "The Mendozas have been doing this for years," he thought. "We can't stop now. So, I'll be alone on Christmas. But those people are alone every day of the year. I like helping them. That's the meaning of Christmas."

Just then the telephone rang.

"Casa Mendoza. Can I help you?" Ramón said.

"Mr. Mendoza, this is Milly from Travel Time. I have good news. I found a room at the Anderson Hotel for three nights. You were right. Some people changed their plans at the last minute. Do you want it?"

"I'm sorry, Milly, but I have changed my plans, too. I forgot. I have to do something very important here on the 25th. I can't leave."

Chapter 7
Suprises

Later that week, Ramón drove Alex to the airport. They didn't say much in the car. Ramón tried to talk, but Alex wasn't interested. They got to the airport, but the plane to Los Angeles was late.

"Well, we'll have to wait for a while," Ramón said. "Do you want to get some ice cream?"

"No, Dad. I don't want any ice cream."

Ramón put his hand on Alex's head.

"Alex, are you sick? You always want ice cream. Something must be wrong." Ramón tried to laugh, but Alex didn't even smile.

"So what do you want to do while we wait?" Ramón said.

Alex said nothing. So they both sat and waited for the plane.

Finally, the plane came and people started getting on. Ramón started to walk onto the plane with Alex. Suddenly, a woman stopped him.

"Do you have a ticket, sir?"

"No," Ramón said. "I'm not going to Los Angeles . . ."

The woman stopped him again. She wasn't very nice. "You can't go on the plane without a ticket."

"But my son is going alone. He's only ten."

Suddenly, the woman was nicer. She smiled at Ramón. "Oh, I'm sorry. I didn't see him there." She looked at Alex. "Hi there. What's your name?"

"Alex." He didn't say anything else.

"Hi, Alex." The woman smiled at Alex, but Alex didn't smile.

Ramón and Alex got on the plane and found Alex's seat. Alex still looked unhappy.

"Don't be like this." Ramón said.

"Don't be like what?"

"Like this is going to be terrible. It's not. You'll have a great time. You'll be back for New Year's, and we'll have Christmas then. OK?"

"Promise?" Alex asked in a small voice.

"Yeah. I promise."

"And do you promise to call me on Christmas Day?"

"Of course I do. And Grandma and Grandpa will call from Mexico, too."

"And you have to promise to give Vincent, Rebecca, and Uncle Alberto their gifts from me . . ."

"Don't worry. I'll do it soon."

"Today."

"I promise. I'll do it today. They'll all have their gifts before you get to your mother's house. Now, I have to go."

He looked at his very unhappy son.

"Hey, how about a smile?"

Alex tried to smile.

"And a smile for your mother when you see her."

"Yeah," Alex said.

"I love you. I'll talk to you on Christmas Day."

Ramón left the airport and immediately went to Vincent's house.

He left Vincent's present with his mother. Then he went to Rebecca's house. She answered the door.

"Ramón. What a nice surprise."

"I just came over to bring you a Christmas present from Alex."

"Alex is so thoughtful. What a good kid!"

"I just put him on the plane to L.A. He's visiting his mother."

"Christmas without Alex! That must be hard for you," Rebecca said.

Ramón didn't say anything.

"Are you OK?" Rebecca asked. "Do you want to come in for a few minutes?"

"OK, but I don't have much time. I have to open the restaurant soon."

He walked into the living room. Rebecca's school books were on the table.

"Hey, you're studying. I should go," he said.

"It's fine. I have a minute."

They both sat down on the sofa.

"Sending Alex to Los Angeles was really hard," Ramón said.

"Of course it was."

"I've never been alone at Christmas," he said.

"Where are your parents?"

"They're in Mexico. I'm all alone in the house."

"At least you'll have your brother here."

"Alberto's going skiing. Aren't you going with him?"

"No, we never talked about it. I don't like skiing."

"Are you doing anything special for Christmas?"

"No, I'll be right here. It'll be just Nancy and me. Are you going to do anything?"

"We have a family tradition. On Christmas Day, we take food to the community center in our neighborhood. My family has been doing it for years. This year I'll have to do it by myself. But it wouldn't be Christmas without it."

Ramón started to get up. "Well, I should go," he said.

"Yeah, and I should study some more."

They walked toward the door. Suddenly Ramón stopped and turned to Rebecca.

"Rebecca, I want to ask you something. Would you spend Christmas with me?"

Rebecca looked surprised.

"Ramón, what can I say?" Rebecca said.

"I . . . I just thought . . . well, you know . . . we're both going to be alone and . . ."

"Ramón, you are a very nice man, and a wonderful father, and I love to . . ."

He stopped her. "I understand. Really, I do. It was a stupid question."

"No, you don't understand, Ramón. Because I'd like to . . ."

But Ramón wasn't listening. He felt stupid. "Why did I do that?" he thought. He started to walk out the door. "Have a great holiday," he said.

Rebecca tried to stop him again. "Wait! Ramón, please understand. It's just that . . ."

"No, I understand. I just, you know . . . No, really, I have to go."

Ramón turned and walked quickly out the door.

* * *

Two days later Ramón took Alberto to the airport for his ski trip. They drove to Alberto's house and picked up his skis. Then Ramón drove his brother to the airport.

"So Rebecca didn't want to go skiing with you?" Ramón asked.

"Well, I never asked her," Alberto said.

"Why not?"

"She wouldn't want to come anyway," Alberto said. "I think she wants to be with somebody else at Christmas."

"Well, maybe next time."

"There won't be a next time, Ramón."

"What? No more skiing?"

"No, no more Rebecca. I'm not dating her anymore."

"You broke up with her?"

"Yeah. Or she broke up with me."

"What do you mean. What happened?"

"Nothing really. We were just talking, and we decided to end it. You know me, Ramón. You said it. I can't stay with one woman very long."

"Well, how is Rebecca? Is she OK?"

"Sure. She's fine. We're still going to be friends. We didn't fight or anything. Don't worry. She doesn't have a broken heart. It's just one of those things. She has school and her music. She's too busy for a relationship. Anyway, she's a nice person, but she's a little too serious for me."

Ramón almost couldn't speak. "Too serious?"

"Yeah. I like to have a good time. But I spent a lot of time trying to understand Rebecca. At first it was OK. But then I didn't like it. I want an easy relationship."

"I see."

"And I have to be honest, Ramón. Rebecca didn't like me enough. I was very good to her, but I never came first in her life. I came after school, her music, her family, her job."

"I don't think that's true, Alberto. Rebecca is trying to do a lot of things right now. This is a very difficult time in her life. Her father just died. She's worried about her brother. She's worried about school. She's worried about money. She cares for you a lot, I'm sure. She just doesn't have much time for a relationship right now."

"Well, that's my point. A relationship needs time. A man needs to feel important. He can't feel like just one more thing in a woman's life."

"We already had this talk once."

"I know. You don't agree with me. Maybe you should go out with Rebecca. She isn't right for me, but maybe she's the right woman for you."

"Maybe she is," Ramón thought.

Chapter 8
Christmas Day

The next day Ramón was working in the kitchen. Suddenly he heard some-one in the restaurant. He walked out and saw Rebecca. She was putting a box of food under the Christmas tree.

"I've always wanted to see Santa Claus," he said.

Rebecca jumped. "Oh, you surprised me. Well, I have to tell the truth. Santa Claus is really a woman."

"I always thought that," Ramón said.

"I want to help with your dinner at the community center. I brought some food, and I can go with you on Christmas Day . . . if you want."

"You can be here on Christmas? Really?"

"Yes, I'd rather be here than any place else. Have you talked to Alex?"

"I talked to him once or twice. He's having a good time, but he wants to come back soon. How's your brother?"

"I got a long letter from him. I'm going to talk to him on Christmas Day."

"This Christmas is going to be pretty good."

"I think so, too," Rebecca said. "What time should I come to the com-munity center?"

"I'll pick you up at 12."

* * *

On Christmas Day, the phone rang early in the morning at Ramón's house. His parents were calling from Mexico.

"Merry Christmas, Ramón!" his mother said.

"Merry Christmas, Mama."

"Were you sleeping?"

"No, I had to get up early today. I have to help Ana with the food for the community center. Are you having a good time?"

"Oh, yes. We've seen almost everyone in the family. We had a wonderful dinner last night at your Aunt Victoria's house. Everyone wished you 'Merry Christmas.' "

"It's Mexican Christmas here, so we already opened our presents. How are you?"

"I'm fine, Mama. I'm going to pick up Rebecca later, and she and I will take the food to the community center. She wants to help."

His mother didn't say anything.

"Mama, are you there?" Ramón asked.

"Yes, I'm here, Ramón. Rebecca's going to help you? Is that OK with Alberto?"

"Don't worry, Mama. Alberto and Rebecca broke up before he left for his ski trip. He thinks Rebecca is too serious. He'll probably meet some new woman on his ski trip. You know Alberto."

"Yes, yes. You're probably right. So, is everything OK? No problems?"

"No problems, Mama. I've already spoken to Alex. He's having a good time. Have you called him yet?"

"No, we haven't. We're going to call him soon."

"Just don't forget. You promised, and he'll remember."

"Don't worry, Ramón. We won't forget. You and Rebecca have a good time today. And wish Rebecca 'Merry Christmas' for us."

"I will, Mama. See you when you get back."

For the first time in years, Ramón felt like singing.

"I'm all alone here," he said. "I can sing if I want to."

So Ramón sang in the shower. He sang while he put on his clothes. He sang while he cooked breakfast.

He went to the restaurant and went into the kitchen. Ana was cooking lots of different foods.

"It smells wonderful in here," Ramón said. "Can I help?"

"No, I'm OK," Ana said. "But you can look for the plastic knives and forks. I can't find them."

Ramón found the plastic knives and forks and put them in a big box.

Fernando walked into the kitchen. He was carrying a big plate of food.

"Fernando, you can go home and have Christmas with your family," Ramón said.

"But you need help. Who will bring the food to the community center?"

"Rebecca wants to help. She's alone at Christmas, too, so she wants to go with us."

"Thanks, Ramón," Fernando said.

At 11:45 A.M., Ramón went to pick up Rebecca.

"Merry Christmas!" she said as she got into the car.

"Merry Christmas!" Ramón said.

"I brought my guitar. I thought we could sing some Christmas songs."

"That's a great idea. Oh, and another 'Merry Christmas' from my parents. They called this morning from Mexico."

"Are they having a good time?"

"Of course. My parents almost always have a good time. They love Mexico. And they love to see their families."

"That's great. I'd like to visit Mexico sometime."

"I'm thinking about taking Alex next summer. He has never been to Mexico."

"Really?" Rebecca said. "I don't believe it. Never?"

"Never. He was too young before. Then after the divorce . . . Well, I just never found the time. I haven't been back to Mexico for 15 years."

"I guess it's not that strange. My family came from Ireland, but I've never been to Ireland."

They stopped at the restaurant and picked up the food. Then they drove to the community center. The center was full. Many of the people were old. There were some families with young children, too. Everyone was smiling.

Many of the people knew Ramón. They said, "Merry Christmas!" to him.

An older woman came up to them. "Do you play the guitar?" she said to Rebecca.

"Yes, I do."

"Can you help us with some Christmas songs? We don't have a piano."

"Sure," Rebecca said. She looked at Ramón.

"Go ahead. I'll bring the food from the car."

Rebecca played her guitar, and everybody sang Christmas songs. Ramón brought the food into the center, and everybody ate. Then they sang more Christmas songs. The children played games and opened presents.

Ramón and Rebecca stayed at the community center for a long time. Finally it was time to go home.

"I'll just take these dirty dishes back to the restaurant," Ramón said.

"Then I'll take you home. You're tired, I know."

"Don't worry about me. I'm fine."

Ramón and Rebecca drove back to the restaurant. They carried the dishes into the kitchen.

"What a day!" Ramón said.

"It was a lot of work. But I really enjoyed it," Rebecca said.

"Would you like a drink?"

"Why not? Christmas only comes once a year."

He filled two glasses. Then he raised his glass. "To a very special Christmas."

Rebecca raised her glass, too. "To a very special person."

"To a great singer."

They both drank their drinks.

"Now this is going to be a perfect day. I'm going to call Alex."

He picked up the telephone and heard it ring at Christine's house.

"Hello, Alex! It's me. Merry Christmas! You got what? Great . . . and what else? Yeah, you have presents here, too. Oh, and someone wants to say hello."

"Merry Christmas, Alex. Yes, it's me. Your dad and I had a great day. He'll tell you all about it. When you get back, we can continue your guitar lessons. Here's your dad."

"You'll be back in a few days," Ramón said to Alex. "I can't wait. It'll be good to see you, too. You're glad because Rebecca's here? Well, I'm glad, too."

Chapter 9

A Perfect Day

After they spoke to Alex, Ramón took Rebecca home.

"Do you want to come in?" Rebecca asked. "Santa Claus left a present here for you."

"Really? He left one for you at my house, too," Ramón said, "but I brought it with me."

They opened the door and walked in. The house was empty.

"Hello? Nancy?" Rebecca called. There was no answer.

"Oh. She must be at the retirement home with her uncle."

"The retirement home?" Ramón asked.

"Yes. He went to live there," Rebecca explained.

"That must be difficult. Especially at Christmas."

"Yeah."

They walked into the living room. Rebecca went over to the Christmas tree and turned the lights on. She picked up some presents and brought them to Ramón.

"Well, you open your gifts first," he said.

Rebecca opened a card from Alex. It said, "Merry Christmas and a Happy New Year. Your friend, Alex."

She opened the present. It was a small statue. On the bottom it said, "Mighty Casey."

"He made it at school," Ramón said.

"Oh! I love it. I'll keep it forever. Now you open my gift."

"A tape! . . . and what could this be?"

"Here. Let me play it for you."

They both listened to Rebecca's song "Dream Catcher."

Ramón listened to the words. "Everybody needs a dream catcher. Dream catcher . . . catch me."

"That was beautiful," Ramón said. "Now you have to open your present from me."

Rebecca opened the gift. It was a small statue of a man.

"What is this?" Rebecca asked.

"It's from Peru. It's called an ekeko," Ramón said.

"I love it!"

"He can bring you good luck. You hang all of your dreams on him, and they'll come true."

There were a few things hanging on the statue. Rebecca pointed to a piece of paper with some words on it. "Is this a diploma?"

"That's for your dream of graduating from music school."

The word *Kevin* was also on a piece of paper. "And Kevin . . ."

"That's for your dream of being with your brother again."

There was also a gold record on the statue. "So the gold record . . ."

"You will sell a million copies of your first record."

"I love it!"

"There's only one problem," Ramón said.

"What's that?"

"If you want your dreams to come true, the ekeko has to smoke every day."

"What?"

"You have to give him one cigarette every day," Ramón explained. He smiled.

"You're kidding, right?"

"No, I'm not."

"Well, Nancy doesn't let people smoke in her house. He'll have to smoke outside."

They both laughed.

Rebecca looked at the fireplace. "Oh look! The fire is almost out."

She got up to fix it. Suddenly, Ramón saw Alberto's picture of him and Alex.

"Alberto's picture. How did it get here?"

"Alberto gave it to me for Christmas."

"It's my favorite picture of Alex."

"It's a great picture of both of you," Rebecca said.

"Let me help you with the fire," Ramón said.

He walked very close to her and helped her with the fire. Ramón burned his hand. Rebecca touched his hand, but he wasn't hurt. He looked into her eyes. Then they kissed.

Suddenly, the door opened. Rebecca's godmother, Nancy, walked into the house.

"Oh, hello. I was wondering about that car in front of the house."

Rebecca and Ramón were both surprised and a little embarrassed.

"Hi, Nancy. You remember Ramón, Alex's father. Ramón, this is my godmother, Nancy Shaw."

"It's nice to see you again," Ramón said.

"I remember now. We met at your parents' retirement party."

"Ramón and I were opening our Christmas presents. Look at my present from Ramón."

She showed her the ekeko and told her the story.

"Well, isn't that something! So he can make all of your dreams come true! Let's hope so."

"Thanks. How's Edward?"

"Not too bad. The retirement home looked great. And we had a delicious dinner. How was your dinner?"

"We had a great time," Rebecca said. "The people at the community center were very happy."

"I do it every year. I really enjoy it," Ramón said. "Listen, I . . . I should go home. Merry Christmas again, Nancy. Happy New Year if I don't see you before then."

Rebecca and Ramón got up.

"Thanks again for the presents," Rebecca said.

"You're welcome. I'll play your tape in the car."

"I'm going to record it again this week. This time it will sound a lot better."

"Your dreams are already coming true. And the ekeko hasn't smoked yet."

Rebecca smiled. She didn't want him to go.

"I'll walk you out," she said. They started walking to the front door.

"I was wondering . . . What are you doing for New Year's?" Ramón asked.

"New Year's Day?"

"No, no. The night before, New Year's Eve."

"I don't have any plans. Why?"

"Well, it's a big night at the restaurant. I have to be there, but it will be fun. If you're not doing anything, you should come. Alex will be there. Can you come?"

"Thank you. I'd love to."

"Great. We'll start the new year together."

He kissed her again. This time they kissed for a long time.

Ramón didn't want to leave. And Rebecca didn't want him to leave. Finally, they stopped kissing, and Ramón left.

Rebecca watched him go. Then she closed the door.

Ramón couldn't believe it. He wanted to run or sing or dance. But he got into the car and started to drive home.

All the way home, he thought about Rebecca. He thought about their Christmas together at the community center. He thought about her present. He thought about their last kiss.

"I can't believe it!" Ramón thought. "She likes me. She likes me a lot. I'm not just Alex's father. I'm not just Alberto's brother. She likes me, Ramón. This is going to be a great new year. I just know it. I'm the luckiest man in the world right now."

Ramón thought of something else and he laughed. "Last week, I was expecting a terrible Christmas. I didn't want to be alone. Well, I'm not alone anymore!" he thought.

"I sound like Alberto when *he* met Rebecca," he thought. "Well, she really is special. Alberto was right. But what will he think about this? I wonder."

Ramón started to think about Alberto's feelings about Rebecca. "Oh, who cares about Alberto?" he thought. "Alberto has probably forgotten about Rebecca already. He probably already met some other woman. Anyway, he said Rebecca wasn't right for him. He was right. Maybe my younger brother does know something about women."

Chapter 10
Missing!

On the day of the New Year's party, Ramón walked into his office in the restaurant. There was a message on the answering machine.

"Hi, Ramón. It's me. I did it! We just recorded my song. I'm very happy with it, and so is my brother, Kevin. I can't wait until you hear it."

"Her brother, Kevin?" Ramón wondered.

Ramón picked up the telephone and called Rebecca.

"Hi! I got your message. That's great news about your song. What was that about Kevin? Is he here?" Ramón asked.

"Yes, he is. My aunt and uncle gave him a plane ticket to San Francisco. Isn't that great?"

"Yes, it is, Rebecca. I'm very happy for you. You see? The ekeko is working already. Your song sounds great, and you and Kevin are together."

"You're right. Listen, I can't give the kids a guitar lesson today. I want to show Kevin around San Francisco. I tried to call the Wangs, but no one answered."

"Don't worry, Rebecca. I have to take Alex there. I'll tell them."

"Thanks a lot, Ramón."

Ramón took Alex to the Wangs'.

"Rebecca's brother is here," he said to Mrs. Wang. "She can't give the boys a lesson today. Maybe they can just practice together."

"That's a good idea," she said.

"I'll pick you up in an hour, Alex. See you later."

When Ramón picked Alex up that afternoon, Alex was a little quiet.

"How was guitar practice?" Ramón asked.

"OK."

"Is something wrong, Alex? Did you have a fight with Vincent?"

"No. Nothing's wrong, Dad. I'm just thinking."

Ramón didn't ask any more questions. He knew his son. Alex would tell him when he was ready.

The afternoon of the New Year's Eve party, Ramón was at the restaurant. He was working hard. Suddenly he heard a voice. He looked up and saw Rebecca and her brother.

"Ramón . . . is this a bad time?" Rebecca asked.

"No, Rebecca, of course not. Come in. This must be Kevin."

"I'm showing Kevin the city."

"It's a great time to be in San Francisco. New Year's is one long party from morning until night," Ramón said.

"Ramón, is it OK if Kevin comes tonight?"

"Of course," Ramón said. "Put on your dancing shoes, Kevin. The band is very good."

"Well, we should go," Rebecca said. "You're very busy. We'll see you later."

"See you later," Ramón said. He started walking back to the kitchen.

Kevin and Rebecca started to leave, but Mr. Wang walked into the restaurant.

"Mr. Wang," Rebecca said. "This is my brother, Kevin. Kevin, I give Mr. Wang's son guitar lessons."

"It's nice to meet you," Kevin said.

"Nice to meet you, too. Have you seen Vincent today?" he asked Rebecca.

Rebecca said *no*. So Mr. Wang went to ask Ramón.

"Should we go?" Kevin asked Rebecca.

"Wait," she said. "Something's wrong."

"Have you seen Vincent?" Mr. Wang asked Ramón.

"No, Vincent hasn't been here all day."

"We can't find him. He didn't come home for lunch, and my wife is very worried. Somebody saw him with Alex."

"That can't be. Alex is home. Let's call him. Maybe he has seen Vincent."

Ramón picked up the telephone to call.

"I got the answering machine," he said. "I'm going to the house. Something could be wrong."

"We'll get a call from them, I'm sure," Mr. Wang said. "My wife is at home waiting. Can somebody wait at your house?"

Ramón started to say no, but Rebecca spoke. "Kevin and I will answer the phone at your house, Ramón," she said.

"That isn't much fun for you," Ramón said.

"It's OK. Those boys are very important to me."

Mr. Wang left. Ramón went to talk to Fernando and the other people in the kitchen. He came back and put his jacket on.

"OK, we can go now," Ramón said.

They drove to Ramón's house without speaking. When they arrived, Ramón ran into the house.

"Alex! Alex!" he called.

"He's not here, Ramón," Rebecca said.

"I'm going to check with my neighbor. Maybe she knows something."

He returned a few minutes later. "She hasn't seen him since early this afternoon," Ramón said.

He picked up the telephone.

"Hello, Mrs. Wang. Alex and Vincent are not here. You haven't heard? . . . Yes, I'll call you when I hear something."

Ramón asked, "What do I do now?"

"Tell Ramón your idea, Kevin."

"Maybe they went out for New Year's? Maybe they just wanted to have a good time."

Suddenly Ramón saw Alex's bag. He looked inside the bag. There was a newspaper in it. Ramón picked it up.

"Look, they cut an ad out of the paper! It's a skating ad. Maybe they went skating."

"You guys go and look for them," Kevin said. "I'll wait here."

"Thanks a lot, Kevin," Ramón said. "Oh, and I almost forgot. The babysitter—she's coming at seven o'clock. There's some money over there. Please give it to her, and apologize for me."

Ramón and Rebecca went to the Embarcadero. They showed Alex's picture to one of the workers.

"Yeah," the man said. "He was here earlier with a friend. He hurt his foot, so he couldn't walk very well. They left about an hour ago."

Rebecca and Ramón went back to the car. They started driving around looking for the boys.

"Maybe they went to the park. Let's look there," Ramón said.

They got out of the car and started to walk through the park.

"Alex . . . Vincent . . . Alex," they shouted.

"I don't see them. They're not here," Ramón said after a few minutes.

"No, they're not. Maybe we should go back home."

They walked through the park and looked for a telephone.

"This is all my fault," Ramón said.

"What do you mean?"

"I haven't been fair to Alex. I've asked him to make a choice—me or his mother. Maybe he should just live with her. I haven't been a very good father." He started to cry.

"Come on, Ramón. I've seen you with Alex. You're a great father. No one could love Alex more than you do."

She hugged him.

"Look, there's a telephone," Rebecca said. "Let's call Kevin. Maybe *he* has heard something."

Ramón put the money into the telephone and called.

". . . They what?" Ramón said. "The hospital? Kevin! Is Alex all right? Where are they? OK. We'll be home soon."

He hung up the telephone and hugged Rebecca.

"What happened?" Rebecca asked. "Are they OK?"

"The Wangs found them," Ramón said. "They were at the hospital. Alex hurt his leg, but he's OK. And Vincent is fine. Mr. Wang is driving them home."

"That's great news," Rebecca said.

* * *

Ramón and Rebecca drove to Ramón's. Mr. Wang and the boys arrived soon after. Ramón hugged and kissed his son. Then he and the Wangs talked alone.

Rebecca stayed with Alex and Vincent in the living room. After a few minutes, Ramón came over to his son.

"Alex, Mr. and Mrs. Wang explained everything to me. You and Vincent were both upset. You don't have to worry about living with me or your mother anymore. She and I are going to work things out. You'll be happy, I promise. OK?"

"Yes, Dad," Alex said.

"Listen, I want us to spend New Year's Eve together. You can come with us to the restaurant. But tomorrow we have to have a long, serious talk about this. You and Vincent upset a lot of people tonight."

"I know, Dad. We won't do it again," Alex said.

Chapter 11

Happy New Year!

Ramón, Rebecca, Alex, and Kevin left the house to go to the restaurant.

Ramón carried Alex in his arms and put him on a chair. Just then Fernando came up to them.

"You found him. Alex, what happened to your ankle?"

"I was skating and I hurt it. But it's going to be OK."

"You went skating?" Fernando asked.

"Don't ask," Ramón said. "I'll tell you about it later."

He looked at the restaurant. There were lots of people. "How's the party? Is everyone having a good time?"

"Yes. It's a great party, Ramón," Fernando said.

"Congratulations! You did a great job without me!"

"Well, it wasn't really that difficult and . . ."

"Fernando. Remember, believe in yourself!"

"Yes, Ramón. Thank you very much, but everyone helped."

* * *

Soon it was almost the end of the year. At 11:59 P.M., everyone started to count.

"Ten . . . nine . . . eight . . . seven . . . six . . . five . . . four . . . three . . . two . . . one . . . Happy New Year!"

Ramón turned to Rebecca, and they kissed.

"This is going to be a very good year," Ramón said to her.

"I think so, too. Happy New Year," Rebecca answered.

A few minutes later, Fernando came over to Kevin and Alex.

"Would you like something to eat or drink?"

"Yes, I would. I'm really thirsty," Alex said.

"Thanks," Kevin said, "but I can get it myself. There are some beautiful young women over there. Maybe I'll go talk to them."

Ramón heard him. "Let me introduce you to them, Kevin." He walked with Kevin to the dance floor and introduced him to some young women.

Rebecca sat at the table with Alex. Fernando came back to the table with some cold drinks. He gave one to Alex and one to Rebecca.

"Here you are, Rebecca. Ramón looks very happy tonight."

"Of course. He found his son."

"Maybe that's not the only reason," he said. He smiled at her.

Rebecca smiled at him, too.

Ramón left Kevin with the young women and walked back to Alex and Rebecca.

"Alex, are you comfortable here?"

"Sure, Dad. I'll be fine."

"Don't worry Ramón. I'll stay with him," Fernando said.

"Well, then Ms. Casey, would you like to dance?" Ramón asked.

"Yes, I would, Mr. Mendoza."

Ramón and Rebecca went to the dance floor. They danced and talked for a long time.

When they got back to the table, Alex was sleeping in the chair.

"Maybe I should take him home," Ramón said. "It's been a long day."

"Where's Kevin?" Rebecca asked.

"He's standing near the band," Ramón said.

Rebecca walked up to Kevin. He was talking to another young man.

"Listen, Ramón wants to take Alex home. He's already sleeping. So I'm sorry, but . . ."

"That's OK, Kevin," the other guy said. "You don't have to go. We can give you a ride."

"No, I should go," Kevin said. "I have to leave tomorrow, and I have to do a lot of things in the morning."

"Are you sure? It's no problem," the guy said.

"I'm sure. But thanks anyway. Maybe I'll see you when I come back to visit again."

Rebecca and Kevin walked back to Ramón.

"Sorry, Kevin. This trip hasn't been very much fun for you."

"No problem. There will be other trips to San Francisco for me."

"That's true. I'll be expecting you next year. Then I can plan some things."

Rebecca and Kevin walked with Ramón to the car. Ramón carried Alex.
"What time is your flight tomorrow, Kevin?" Rebecca asked.
"It leaves at 3:30."
"Really?" Ramón said. "My parents are coming back from Mexico at four
o'clock. I could take you to the airport."
"You don't have to do that, Ramón," Rebecca said. "Nancy is planning
to take us."
"That's silly," Ramón said. "I have to go anyway. It's no trouble."
"That's great," Kevin said. "Thanks."
"But what about Alex?" Rebecca asked. "He can't walk. He needs help."
"I already called the babysitter for tomorrow."
"All right then. Thanks a lot," Rebecca said.
"I'll pick you up at two o'clock. Is that OK?" Ramón asked.
"That sounds good," Rebecca said.
Ramón stopped the car at Nancy's house, and Rebecca and Kevin got
out of the car. Ramón walked to the door with them.
"Thanks a lot, Ramón," Kevin said.
"Thank you, Kevin," Ramón said. "You were a big help."
"No problem. A month ago, I was a big problem. Now I'm a big help. I
like that." He smiled and walked into the house.
After Kevin went in, Rebecca talked to Ramón. "Kevin has really
changed," she said. "He has really grown up a lot."
"Well, I didn't know him before, but he's a pretty good kid now," Ramón
said.
"The farm has been good for him."
Ramón put his arms around Rebecca. "You were pretty good for him,
too," he said.
"I tried. But it was hard. He never really had a mother. I tried to do a lot
for him. But now he doesn't have a father, either. The farm has helped a lot.
He really likes my Uncle Brendan. He even likes milking cows."
"So does he want to be a farmer now?"
"No. I don't think so. He still likes computers. He's thinking about
coming to San Francisco to study computers."
"That would be great for him and for you," Ramón said
"Yeah. Well, we'll see. Hey, you should go home. Alex is waiting for
you."
"You're right. Thank you for everything, Rebecca. You were great." They
kissed.
"Thank you, too, Ramón."
"For what?" he asked.
"For letting me be part of your life," she answered.
They kissed again.

Chapter 12
Goodbye

The next day, Ramón arrived at Nancy's house at two o'clock.

"You're right on time," Rebecca said. Ramón just smiled.

Kevin carried his suitcase out to the car. Nancy came out to say goodbye.

"Thanks a lot, Nancy," Kevin said. "It was nice to meet you."

"It was nice to meet you, too, Kevin. Finally. Your mother would be very proud of you."

She hugged him. Then he and Rebecca got into the car.

"Ramón's parents are arriving at four o'clock, so I won't be home until after five," Rebecca said to Nancy.

"Wait a minute, Rebecca. Aren't you coming to my house for dinner? I'm making a big meal for my parents. Can you come?"

Rebecca looked at Nancy. Nancy smiled at her. "It's OK, Rebecca. I'm having dinner with my neighbor Ruth tonight. Don't worry about me."

Rebecca turned to Ramón again. "OK. I would love to have dinner with you and your parents, Ramón."

Ramón drove them to the airport. Kevin went to the desk and showed the woman his ticket. Then he gave her his suitcase.

"Everything is fine, Mr. Casey," the woman said. "Your flight is leaving in 45 minutes. You can get on the plane soon. Please wait at Gate 17."

"Can my friends wait with me?" he asked.

"No, I'm sorry," she said. "They can't go to the gate without a ticket."

Kevin went back to the car to talk to Ramón and Rebecca.

"They won't let you come to the gate," Kevin said.

"You stay here with Kevin," Ramón said. "I have to park the car, so I'll say goodbye now."

"Thanks for everything, Ramón. And don't let my sister work too hard."

"Bye, Kevin." They shook hands. Then Ramón left.

Kevin and Rebecca walked into the airport again. "I had a really good time," he said.

Rebecca hugged her brother. "Take care of yourself, Kevin. And give my love to Aunt Anne and Uncle Brendan."

"Don't worry. I will. You take care of yourself, too."

"It was great seeing you, Kevin. I'll call next weekend," Rebecca said.

"Fine. I'll be waiting."

He kissed her and walked toward the gate. Rebecca watched him. She was crying a little.

Ramón came back and found Rebecca. She was still sad.

"Don't worry," Ramón said. "You'll see him again soon."

"I know," she said.

"Well, we have about an hour. Would you like to go to get cup of coffee?" Ramón said.

"That sounds good."

They found a small restaurant in the airport. They went in and sat down.

"Two coffees, please," Ramón said to the waiter.

Ramón took Rebecca's hand.

"Are you OK?"

"Sure. I'm fine."

"You aren't worried about Kevin, are you?"

"No, he's going to be fine. I know that. I just want to see him more. That's all."

"I know. I've always had my family near me. It must be very difficult for the two of you."

"Yes. Kevin and I have always been very close. We don't have any other family now."

"You have your aunt and uncle now."

"That's true. We lost our father, but we got two people in return."

"Big families are hard, too," Ramón said. "I have lots of aunts and uncles. I can never remember their names. And I'm better than Alberto. He can't remember anyone's name!" Ramón said.

Ramón looked at Rebecca when he said his brother's name.

"You know, Ramón, we haven't talked about Alberto," she said.

"I know. We need to talk about him. But I'm a little afraid."

"What are you afraid of?"

"I don't know. You broke up with him. But do you still have feelings for him?"

"No. I did before, but now he's just a friend. I care about him, but I care about Alex and your mother and father, too."

Ramón took a deep breath. "That's good. You really are special."

"Why did you ask?"

"Well, most women like Alberto better."

"I don't believe that," Rebecca said.

"It's true."

"Even your ex-wife?"

"Well, maybe not Christine. She never liked anyone in my family very much. But most other women like Alberto better."

"I can't understand that. Alberto is very good-looking, and he's a lot of fun. But you're much more than that. You understand me. Alberto never understood about school or about my music. But you always understood. That's very important to me. When I got back from Boston, I knew. My relationship with Alberto just wasn't working."

"I always liked you," Ramón said. "I even wrote you a letter when you were back in Boston. I told you my feelings. But I never sent it. I couldn't. Alberto is my brother. You were his girlfriend. It just wasn't right."

"Well, it's all right now."

"I hope so. But there may still be a problem."

"Why?" she asked.

"Well, he told me to ask you out. But I don't think he meant it. He may still have feelings for you."

"I don't think so, Ramón. I'm not right for Alberto."

"He said that, too. But I don't know. I care for you so much. It's just difficult to believe him."

Rebecca laughed.

* * *

At four o'clock they went downstairs to wait for Mr. and Mrs. Mendoza.

"We can meet them here. They have to pick up their suitcases here," Ramón said to Rebecca.

After about 15 minutes, they saw Ramón's parents. They walked over to them. Ramón hugged them.

"Welcome back!" he said.

"We're happy to be back," Mr. Mendoza said. "It's nice to go away, but it's even nicer to come home."

"Rebecca," Mrs. Mendoza said, "this is a surprise." She hugged Rebecca, too.

"Rebecca's brother had a flight about half an hour ago, so I gave him a ride," Ramón explained.

"Rebecca and I will get the car," Ramón said. "Mama, you and Papa should wait here."

Rebecca and Ramón went to get the car. "This feels very strange," Rebecca said. "Maybe I shouldn't go to dinner at your house?"

"Don't be silly. Everything will be fine. My mother is just surprised. That's all."

Ramón picked up his parents and they drove home.

"So, how was everything here?" Mr. Mendoza asked.

"Well, we had a little problem yesterday. I'll tell you about it at dinner."

They walked into the house. Suddenly the telephone rang. Mrs. Mendoza answered it.

"Oh, Alberto. We just got home. Are you having a good time?"

"Why should I sit down? Is something wrong?" she asked. She sat down.

"What? You're bringing her here? You want her to meet us? Tomorrow? OK. See you then, Son."

She hung up the telephone.

"I don't believe it. Alberto has met someone . . . a woman. He said she's the right woman for him. She's from San Jose. They're coming back together tomorrow."

Ramón put his arm around Rebecca.

"That's great news, Mama. I can't wait to meet her!"